WHY LEARN CURSIVE HANDWRITING?

In the modern world of typing and instant messaging, writing with pen and paper, let alone in cursive script, may seem like a thing of the past. However, researchers believe that cursive handwriting is important to cognitive development and the sensorimotor region of the brain. That is especially true for young children.

5 BENEFITS OF CURSIVE HANDWRITING

1. Improves the Process of Learning
When children learn a language, they usually learn in one form. By learning to write in a cursive way, they can get one more opportunity to learn the alphabets, words, and sentences.

2. Boosts Motor Skills Development
Cursive handwriting is a form of creative writing that requires more focus, practice, and discipline than a regular way of writing. While practicing it, the hand muscles of children are used differently and stimulate the part of the brain which sharpens their motor skills.

3. Makes Children Smarter
According to memory experts and researchers, cursive handwriting can help a child to become more intelligent. Writing with hands propels your brain to integrate different inputs such as tactile and visual information simultaneously while using fine motor skills.

4. Emboldens Children With Learning Disabilities
Children with dyslexia and other learning disabilities find it difficult to write in print format as they perceive many letters as being similar. Cursive letters look way different from print letters. They open up another option for children with disabilities. It ultimately helps them overcome their disability and feel more confident.

5. Enables Faster Speed of Writing
Writing with a good speed means finishing exams wit[...] timeframe while covering all the possible questions. Cur[...] helps children to write faster than the regular style of p[...] requires you to lift your pen less often. It's been observed [...] faster writing speed have a better attention span while writing.

HOW TO USE THIS BOOK

This cursive handwriting workbook consists of three parts:

1. Cursive Handwriting Crash Course

If your child is completely new to cursive handwriting this section will jump-start her learning process. The course starts with the basic strokes and then progresses to the letters that are based on these strokes. As soon as the child learns how to write her first letters the course would provide an opportunity to write some words with them. This way your child's newly acquired skills would stick better. The course starts with lowercase letters and then moves to the uppercase ones. At the end of the course your child will find some pangrams (sentences that contain all the letters of the alphabet) to practice on.

2. Sentences Writing Practice

This chapter provides additional sentences to practice on. Each sentence focuses on a particular letter of the alphabet.

3. Blank Writing Practice Sheets

Here your child will have some space to write her own words and sentences using the skills acquired from this workbook.

We are happy to receive any of your feedback regarding this workbook at:
lilas.publishing@ya.ru

Lilas Lingvo Team

CONTENTS

Cursive handwriting Crash Course

Lesson 1: Wave strokes

Let's start our journey to cursive mastery by learning to write 'wave' strokes (thus called as they resemble little waves). First let's try writing short wave strokes.

This is one of the basic cursive strokes that we'll use later to write several different letters.

Now let's learn how to write tall wave strokes.

Lesson 2: Letters 'i', 's', 'r' and 't'

Let's learn how to turn short and long wave strokes into letters 'i', 's', 'r' and 't' starting with 'i'. Make your short wave stroke and then dot each spike:

Let's write the letter 'i' separately. Start a short wave stroke and stop between the bottom line and the middle line. Dot the spikes:

Now we'll turn a short wave stroke into the letter 's'. Start a short wave stroke, open it up, bring it up to almost touch the wave, then pull it back up and start again:

Let's write the letter 's' separately. Start a short wave stroke, open it up, almost touch the wave, pull it back up, give it a little tail and stop:

Let's turn a short wave stroke into the letter 'r'. Start a short wave, stop at the middle line, make a little curve, bring it down and then pull back up to the middle line:

Let's write the letter 'r' separately. Start a short wave stroke, stop at the middle line, make a little curve, bring it down, then stop half way between the bottom and the middle lines:

Now we are going to use a long wave stroke to write the letter 't'. Make a long wave stroke almost to the top line, then cross the tall spikes right on the middle line:

Now let's write the letter 't' separately. Make a long wave stroke almost to the top line, pull it down, stop between the bottom line and the middle line, then cross the spike right on the middle line:

Lesson 3: Words with letters 'i', 's', 'r' and 't'

In this lesson you will practice writing words with cursive using the letters that you've learnt. Practice writing these words until you'll get comfortable writing them. Try to keep consistent slant using the slant guides:

sit sit sit sit sit sit sit

sit sit sit sit sit sit sit

its its its its its its its

its its its its its its its

stin stin stin stin stin stin

stin stin stin stin stin stin

sin sin sin sin sin sin sin

sin sin sin sin sin sin sin

tis tis tis tis tis tis tis

tis tis tis tis tis tis tis

Lesson 4: Short curved wave stroke

In this lesson you will learn how to write a short curved wave stroke. It is similar to the short wave stroke that we've learnt only there is a small curve at the top of it.

Lesson 5: Letters 'a', 'o', 'd', 'g' and 'c'

In this lesson you will learn how to write letters 'a', 'o', 'd', 'g' and 'c' using a short curved wave stroke.

Let's start with the letter 'a'. Make a curved wave stroke as usual only at the end bring the bottom stroke up to touch the tip of the curved wave and then pull back down:

Now let's write the letter 'a' separately. Make a curved wave stroke, bring the bottom stroke up to touch the tip of curve and give it a little tail:

Let's turn a curved wave stroke into the letter 'o'. Make a curved wave stroke, bring the bottom stroke up to touch the tip of the curve, make a little loop at the top of the letter and give it a little link from there:

Now let's write letter 'o' separately. Make a curved wave stroke, bring the bottom stroke up to touch the tip of the curve, make a little loop at the top of the letter and give it a little link from there:

Let's write the letter 'd' using the curved wave stroke. Make a curved wave stroke, bring the bottom stroke up, touch the tip of the top curve, bring the stroke almost all the way up to the top line, then bring it down and start all over again:

Now let's write the letter 'd' separately. Make a curved wave stroke, bring the bottom stroke up to the tip of the top curve, then all the way up to the top line, then down and give it a little tail:

Let's turn a curved wave stroke into the letter 'g'. Make a curved wave stroke, bring the bottom stroke up to touch the tip of the curve, then bring it down below the bottom line and make a loop and then go up:

Now let's write the letter 'g' separately. Make a curved wave stroke, bring the bottom stroke up to touch the tip of the curve, then bring it down below the bottom line and make a loop and go up:

Let's turn a curved wave stroke into the letter 'c'. It is just the same as the curved wave stoke itself. When you're making a curved wave stroke you're making the letter 'c':

Now let's write the letter 'c' separately. Make a curved wave stroke, pull it up half way between the bottom line and the middle line and stop:

Lesson 6: Words with letters 'a', 'o', 'd', 'g' and 'c'

In this lesson you will practice writing words with cursive using the letters that you've learnt so far. Practice writing these words until you'll get comfortable writing them:

dog dog dog dog dog

dog dog dog dog dog

toad toad toad toad

toad toad toad toad

got got got got got got

got got got got got got

road road road road

road road road road

cod cod cod cod cod cod

cod cod cod cod

cod

nag nag nag nag nag nag

nag nag nag nag nag nag

door door door door door

door door door door door

god god god god god god

god god god god god god

Lesson 7: Cursive hill stroke

In this lesson we are going to practice the 'cursive hill stroke'. Make sure that the top of the 'hill' touches the middle line:

Lesson 8: Letters 'm' and 'n'

Let's turn the hill stroke into the letters 'm' and 'n'. Let's start with 'm'. First create a little tail, make two hill strokes, then pull the stroke up and start again:

Now let's write the letter 'm' separately. Start with a little tail, make two hill strokes and then finish with a little tail:

Writing the letter 'n' is very similar to 'm'. Start with a little tail, make one hill stroke, then pull the stroke back up and start again:

Now let's write the letter 'n' separately. Start with a little tail, make one hill stroke and then finish with a little tail:

Finally, let's put letters 'm' and 'n' together. Try not to get confused between them!

Lesson 9: Words with letters 'm' and 'n'

In this lesson you will practice writing words using letters and strokes that you've learnt so far. Practice writing these words until you'll get comfortable writing them:

man man man man

man man man man

moon moon moon moon

moon moon moon moon

moon moon moon

moon moon moon

noam noam noam noam

noam noam noam noam

main main main main

main main main main

Lesson 10: Letters 'u' and 'w'

In this lesson we are going to use the short wave stroke again to practice writing letters 'u' and 'w'. Let's start with 'u'. Make a short wave stroke, make a connection and start again:

Now let's write the letter 'u' separately. Make a short wave stroke, then another short wave stroke and then end it:

Let's use the short wave stroke to write the letter 'w'.
Make three short wave strokes and the add a little link to
the next letter:

Now let's write
the letter 'w'
separately. Make
three short wave
strokes and then
leave a little curve
as the tail:

Lesson 11: Words with letters 'u' and 'w'

In this lesson we are going to use the short wave stroke again to practice writing letters 'u' and 'w'. Let's start with 'u'. Make a short wave stroke, then stretch the next stroke a little further and then start again:

mug mug mug mug

mug mug mug mug

narrow narrow narrow

narrow narrow narrow

nvag nvag nvag nvag nvag

nvag nvag nvag nvag nvag

nv nv nv nv nv nv nv nv

nv nv nv nv nv nv nv nv

stranv stranv stranv stranv

stranv stranv stranv stranv

Lesson 12: Short loop and long loop strokes

In this lesson you will learn two new strokes: the short loop stroke and the long loop stroke. Let's start with the short loop. Start at the bottom line and make even loops that reach the middle line:

The tall loop is similar only you pull the stroke all the way to the top line. Try to make straight nice looking loops:

Lesson 13: Letters 'e', 'l' and 'b'

In this lesson you will practice turning the short loop stroke into the letter 'e'. In fact the short loop stroke is a ready letter 'e'. Let's practice writing it again:

Now let's practice writing the letter 'e' separately. Maka a single short loop stroke and end it with a little tail:

Let's use the long loop stroke to create the letter 'l'. The way to do it is just writing long loop strokes:

Now let's practice writing the letter 'l' separately. Make a single long loop stroke and end it with a little tail:

Let's use the long loop stroke to create the letter 'b'. First make a long loop stroke as usual, pull it up to the middle line, make a small loop, then pull the stoke to the right and start a new long loop stroke:

Now let's practice writing letter 'b' separately. Make a long loop stroke, pull it up to the middle line, make a small loop, then pull to the right:

Lesson 14: Words with letters 'e', 'l' and 'b'

In this lesson you will practice writing words using letters and strokes that you've learnt so far. Practice writing these words until you'll get comfortable writing them:

ball ball ball ball ball

ball ball ball ball ball

lonesome lonesome

lonesome lonesome

bleed bleed bleed bleed

bleed bleed bleed bleed

alone alone alone alone

alone alone alone alone

secure secure secure secure

secure secure secure secure

babble babble babble

able able able able able

lecture lecture lecture

Lesson 15: Letters 'k', 'h' and 'f'

In this lesson you will be turning the long loop stroke into the letters 'k', 'h' and 'f'.

Let's start with 'k'. Make a long loop stroke, stop at the bottom line, come back up to the middle line with a little arch, make a little loop there and then pull the stroke out:

Now let's practice writing the letter 'k' separately. Make a long loop stroke, stop at the bottom line, come back up to the middle line with a little arch, make a little loop and then pull the stroke out:

Let's turn the long loop stroke into the letter 'h'. Make a long loop stroke, stop at the bottom and then make a hill. Come back up, make another loop and make a hill again:

Now let's practice writing the letter 'h' separately. Make a long loop stroke, stop at the bottom and then make a hill. End with a little tail:

Let's use the long loop stroke to make the letter 'f'. Start a long loop stroke and when you come down go below the bottom line, make a loop at the bottom touching the stroke where it crosses the bottom line and then start a new long loop stroke:

Now let's write the letter 'f' separately. Start a long loop stroke and when you come down go below the bottom line, make a loop at the bottom and then end with a little tail:

Lesson 16: Words with letters 'k', 'h' and 'f'

In this lesson you will practice writing words using letters and strokes that you've learnt so far. Practice writing these words until you'll get comfortable writing them:

hoof hoof hoof hoof hoof

hoof hoof hoof hoof hoof

knife knife knife knife

knife knife knife knife

hike hike hike hike hike

hike hike hike hike hike

flock flock flock flock

flock flock flock flock

knock knock knock

knock knock knock

bleak bleak bleak bleak

bleak bleak bleak bleak

hook hook hook hook

hook hook hook hook

fake fake fake fake fake

fake fake fake fake fake

Lesson 17: Letter 'q'

In this lesson you will learn how to write the letter 'q' using the curved wave stroke. Make a curved wave stroke, touch the tip of the wave at the top like when writing the letter 'a', then pull down below the bottom line and make a loop that touches the stroke right where it crosses the bottom line. Then keep going and start a new curved wave stroke:

Now let's practice writing letter 'q' separately:

Lesson 18: Words with the letter 'q'

In this lesson you will practice writing words using letters and strokes that you've learnt so far. Practice writing these words until you'll get comfortable writing them:

quit quit quit quit quit

quit quit quit quit quit

agua agua agua agua

agua agua agua agua

quake quake quake quake

quake quake quake quake

quorum quorum quorum

quorum quorum quorum

equal equal equal equal

equal equal equal equal

Lesson 19: Short wave loop stroke

In this lesson you will learn how to write the 'short wave loop stroke'. Start writing the short wave stroke. When you reach the middle line pull it down below the bottom line and make a loop to the left. Pull the stroke back up and cross the stroke at the bottom line:

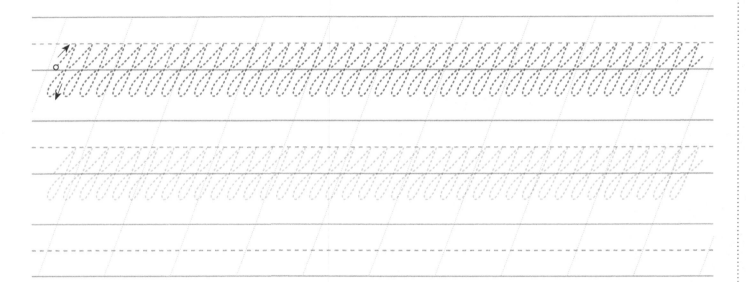

48

Lesson 20: Letters 'j', 'p' and 'y'

In this lesson you will be using the short wave loop stroke to write the letters 'j', 'p' and 'y'. Let's start with 'j'. Simply make the short wave loop stroke and then put the dots above the spikes:

Now let's practice writing the letter 'j' separately. Make a short wave loop stroke and when you pull the stroke above the bottom line end it with a little tail:

Let's use the short wave loop stroke to write the letter 'p'. Make a short wave loop stroke only instead of making a loop below the bottom line, pull the stroke straight back up, make a loop between the bottom line and the middle line, pull the stroke right and start again:

Now let's practice writing the letter 'p' separately. Start a short wave loop stroke, pull it straight back up, make a loop between the bottom line and the middle line and pull a little tail to the right:

Let's use the short wave loop stroke to write the letter 'y'. We start the letter 'y' with a short wave stroke and then a short wave loop stroke. Cross the stroke at the bottom line:

Now let's practice writing the letter 'y' separately. Start with a short wave stroke, then a short wave loop stroke. Cross the stroke at the bottom line and end with a little tail:

Lesson 21: Words with letters 'j', 'p' and 'y'

In this lesson you will practice writing words using letters and strokes that you've learnt so far. Practice writing these words until you'll get comfortable writing them:

jumpy jumpy jumpy

jumpy jumpy jumpy

popinjay popinjay

popinjay popinjay

pyjamas pyjamas

pyjamas pyjamas

jeepney jeepney jeepney

jeepney jeepney jeepney

pay pay pay pay pay

pay pay pay pay pay

Lesson 22: Letters 'z', 'v' and 'x'

In this lesson you will learn how to write the cursive letters 'z', 'v' and 'x'. Let's start with the letter 'z'. Make a hill stroke, then pull the stroke below the bottom line and make a loop there crossing the initial stroke at the bottom line:

Now let's practice writing letter 'z' separately:

Let's learn how to write the letter 'v'.
Start with a little hill, make a curve at
the bottom line, come back up and finish
with a little tail. Letter 'v' is somewhat
similar to the letter 'o' only with a gap at
the top:

Now let's practice writing the letter 'v' separately. Start
with a little hill, make a curve at the bottom line, come
back up and finish with a little tail:

Now we'll learn how to write the letter 'x'. Start with a little hill, after you reach the bottom line pull the stroke up and leave a little tail. Then cross that stroke with a straight line from the upper right side to the lower left. Then start a new hill:

Now let's practice writing the letter 'x' separately. Start with a little hill, after you reach the bottom line pull the stroke up and leave a little tail. Then cross that stroke with a straight line from the upper right side to the lower left:

Lesson 23: Words with letters 'z', 'v' and 'x'

In this lesson you will practice writing words using letters and strokes that you've learnt so far. Practice writing these words until you'll get comfortable writing them:

crazy crazy crazy

crazy crazy crazy

wizard wizard wizard

wizard wizard wizard

nex nex nex nex nex

nex nex nex nex nex

savvy savvy savvy

savvy savvy savvy

goo goo goo goo goo goo

goo goo goo goo goo goo

Congratulations! You've now learnt how to write all the lowercase letters of the alphabet in cursive! Let's continue our journey and move on to capital letters!

Lesson 24: Long curved wave stroke

In this lesson you will learn how to write a long curved wave stroke. It is similar to the short curved stroke that you've learnt only it reaches the top line:

Lesson 25: Uppercase letters 'C', 'A' and 'O'

In this lesson you will learn how to write uppercase letters 'C', 'A' and 'O'. These letters look very similar to their lowercase counterparts. Let's start with the letter 'C'. Simply make a single long curved wave stroke:

Now let's continue with the letter 'A'. Start at the top line, make a curved wave stroke, touch the beginning of the stroke and then come back down:

Let's learn how to write the letter 'O'. Start at the top line, make a curved wave stroke, touch the beginning of the stroke, then make a little loop and pull the stroke to the right:

Lesson 26: Words with letters 'C', 'A' and 'O'

In this lesson you will practice writing words using letters and strokes that you've learnt so far. Practice writing these words until you'll get comfortable writing them:

Chicago Chicago Chicago

Chicago Chicago Chicago

Austin Austin Austin

Austin Austin Austin

Cape Cod Cape Cod

Cape Cod Cape Cod

Akron Akron Akron

Akron Akron Akron

Chico Chico Chico Chico

Chico Chico Chico Chico

Letter 'O' is unusual as it ends with a tail close to the top line. The loop that it ends with changes when you need to connect the uppercase 'O' with other lowercase letters. Let's practice writing some words with this type of connection:

Oregon Oregon Oregon

Oregon Oregon Oregon

Omaha Omaha Omaha

Omaha Omaha Omaha

Ozark Ozark Ozark

Ozark Ozark Ozark

Oshkosh Oshkosh Oshkosh

Oshkosh Oshkosh Oshkosh

Overlea Overlea Overlea

Overlea Overlea Overlea

Lesson 27: Long wave stroke

In Lesson 1 you've already practiced writing long wave strokes. There are a number of uppercase letters that you can write using that type of stroke too. But first let's revise writing the long wave stroke itself:

Lesson 28: Uppercase letters 'U', 'Y' and 'V'

In this lesson you will learn how to write uppercase letters 'U', 'Y' and 'V'. Let's start with the letter 'U'. Start with a little tail near the top line, make a long wave stroke and finish with a little tail:

Now let's practice writing the letter 'Y'. Start with a little tail near the top line, make a long wave stroke, pull the stroke down below the bottom line, make a loop to the left, cross the stroke at the bottom line and finish with a little tail:

Now let's practice writing the letter 'V'. Start with a little tail near the top line, make a long wave stroke and stop at the top line:

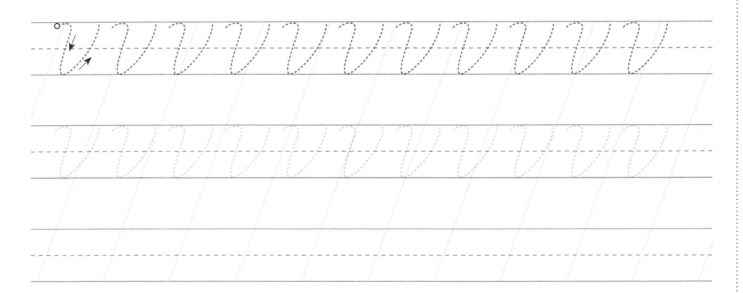

Lesson 29: Words with letters 'U', 'Y' and 'V'

In this lesson you will practice writing words using letters and strokes that you've learnt so far. Practice writing these words until you'll get comfortable writing them:

Yukon Yukon Yukon

Yukon Yukon Yukon

Utica Utica Utica Utica

Utica Utica Utica Utica

Ukiah Ukiah Ukiah

Ukiah Ukiah Ukiah

Yonkers Yonkers Yonkers

Yonkers Yonkers Yonkers

Uvalde Uvalde Uvalde

Uvalde Uvalde Uvalde

Letter 'V' is unusual as it ends at the top line. To connect it with lowercase letters we will have to introduce a loop just like we did with the letter 'O' before. Let's practice writing some words with this type of connection:

Virginia Virginia

Virginia Virginia

Venice Venice Venice

Venice Venice Venice

Vancouver Vancouver

Vancouver Vancouver

Vernon Vernon Vernon

Vernon Vernon Vernon

Visalia Visalia Visalia

Visalia Visalia Visalia

Lesson 30: Uppercase letters 'T', 'F' and 'S'

In this lesson you will learn how to write uppercase letters 'T', 'F' and 'S'. Let's start with the letter 'T'. It consists of two strokes. Start close to the top line and make a vertical stroke to the bottom line, pull it to the left and make a little hook. Then make a wavy stroke on the top of the vertical stroke:

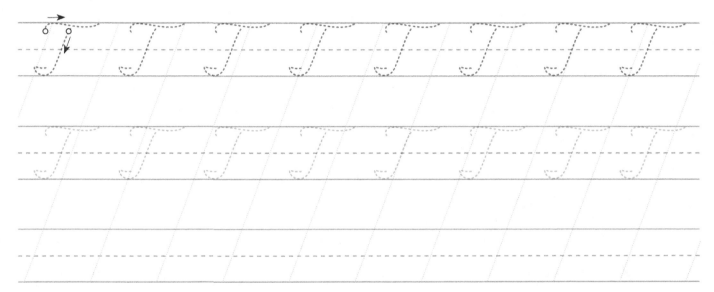

Now let's practice writing the letter 'F'. It consists of three strokes. Start with a 'T' then make a small horizontal stroke at the middle line:

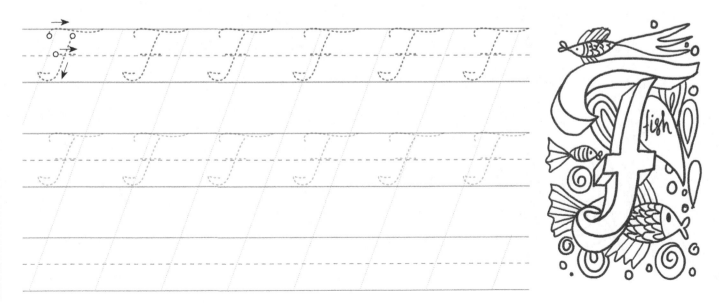

Let's practice writing the letter 'S. It is a one-stroke letter. Start at the bottom line, curve up to the top line, make a loop that crosses itself at the middle line, touch the bottom line, then curve to the left across the initial stroke and make a little hook:

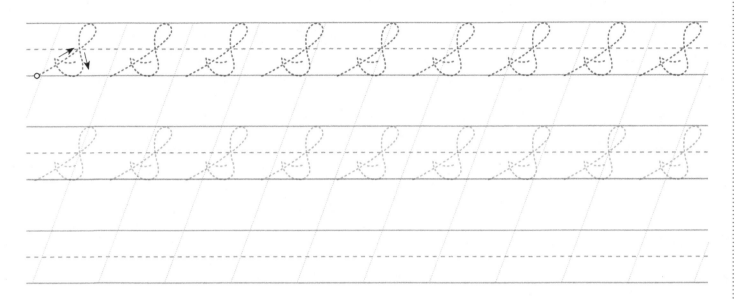

74

Lesson 31: Words with uppercase letters 'T', 'F' and 'S'

The common element of uppercase letters 'T', 'F' and 'S' is that little hook at the end. This hook is used to connect them to lowercase letters. Let's practice writing some words with this type of connection. Add horizontal strokes to 'T' and 'F' after you've written the whole word:

Tampa Tampa Tampa

Tampa Tampa Tampa

Fresno Fresno Fresno

Fresno Fresno Fresno

Seattle Seattle Seattle

Seattle Seattle Seattle

Tucson Tucson Tucson

Tucson Tucson Tucson

Fargo Fargo Fargo

Fargo Fargo Fargo

Lesson 32: Cursive long hill stroke

In this lesson we are going to practice the 'cursive long hill stroke'. It is similar to the cursive hill stroke that we've practiced before only the long one touches the top line:

Lesson 33: Uppercase letters 'H', 'K', 'M' and 'N'

In this lesson you will learn how to write uppercase letters 'H', 'K', 'M' and 'N'. Let's start with the letter 'H'. This letter requires two strokes. Start with a small hook near the top line, then bring the stroke down to the bottom line. Then start the second stroke at the top line, bring it down to the bottom line, then make a loop that touches the first stroke and pull it to the right:

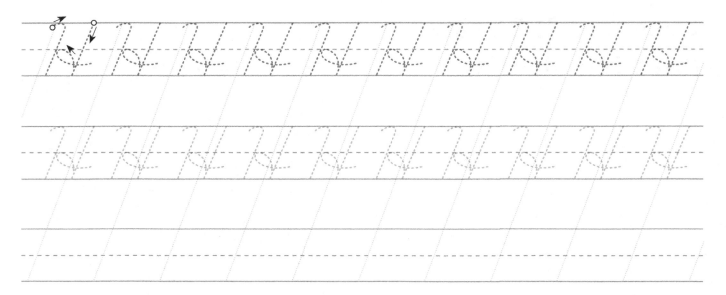

Now let's practice writing the letter 'K'.
It consists of two strokes. Start with a
small hook near the top line, then bring
the stroke down to the bottom line.
Then start the second stroke at the
top line, pull it to the first stroke at the
middle line, then pull it to the right with
a little hook:

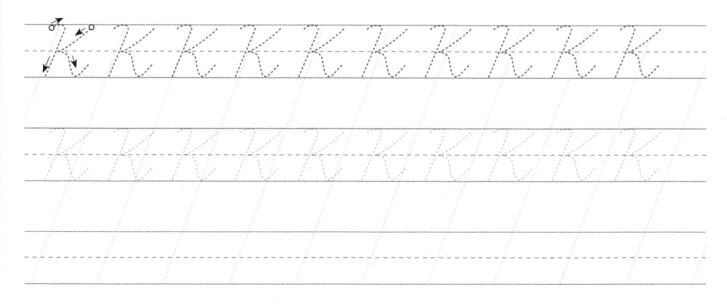

Now let's practice writing the letter 'M'. Start with small
hook near the top line, make two long hill strokes and
finish with a little tail:

Now let's practice writing the letter 'N'. Start with small hook near the top line, make a long hill stroke and finish with a little tail:

NNNNNNNNN

Lesson 34: Words with uppercase letters 'H', 'K', 'M' and 'N'

In this lesson you will practice writing words using letters and strokes that you've learnt so far. Practice writing these words until you'll get comfortable writing them:

Houston Houston

Houston Houston

Killeen Killeen Killeen

Killeen Killeen Killeen

Mesa Mesa Mesa Mesa

Mesa Mesa Mesa Mesa

Newark Newark Newark

Newark Newark Newark

Miami Miami Miami

Miami Miami Miami

Hemet Hemet Hemet

Hemet Hemet Hemet

Kansas Kansas Kansas

Kansas Kansas Kansas

Norfolk Norfolk Norfolk

Norfolk Norfolk Norfolk

Hoover Hoover Hoover

Hoover Hoover Hoover

Kailua Kailua Kailua

Kailua Kailua Kailua

Lesson 35: Uppercase letters 'B', 'P' and 'R'

In this lesson you will learn how to write uppercase letters 'B', 'P', and 'R'. Let's start with the letter 'B'. Start with small hook near the top line, pull down to the bottom line, pull back along the same stroke, make a curve to the middle line, then another curve to the bottom line and finish with a little hook:

Now let's practice writing the letter 'P'. Start like the letter 'B' but finish the last curve at the middle line:

Now let's practice writing the letter 'P'. Start with small hook near the top line, pull down to the bottom line, pull back along the same stroke, make a curve to the middle line, then pull the stroke to the right with an upward curve:

Lesson 36: Words with uppercase letters 'B', 'P' and 'R'

In this lesson you will practice writing words using letters and strokes that you've learnt so far. Pay attention to how uppercase letters connect the lowercase ones. Practice writing these words until they become easy to write:

Boston Boston Boston

Boston Boston Boston

Provo Provo Provo

Provo Provo Provo

Raleigh Raleigh Raleigh

Raleigh Raleigh Raleigh

Buffalo Buffalo Buffalo

Buffalo Buffalo Buffalo

Plano Plano Plano

Plano Plano Plano

Roswell Roswell Roswell

Roswell Roswell Roswell

Bayonne Bayonne

Bayonne Bayonne

Portland Portland

Portland Portland

Lesson 37: Uppercase letters 'G', 'L' and 'Q'

In this lesson you will learn how to write uppercase letters 'G', 'L', and 'Q'. Let's start with the letter 'G'. Start with an upward curve, make a small loop below the top line, curve to the right, then pull down with a curve to the left and finish with a little hook:

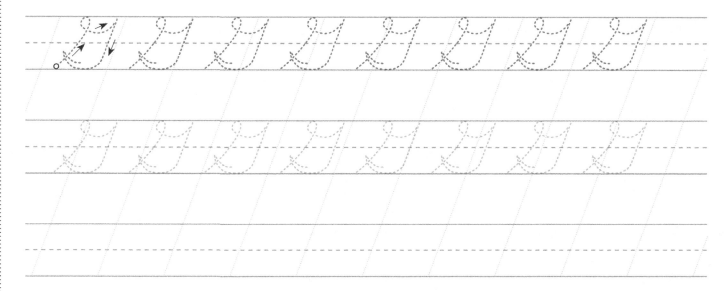

Now let's practice writing the letter 'L'. Start above the middle line, pull the curve to the right, make a small loop below the top line, then pull down and to the left, make a loop and finish with a little tail:

Now let's practice writing the letter 'Q'. Start slightly below the middle line, make a big arch that touches the top line, pull down and to the left to the bottom line, make a small loop and finish with a tail:

Lesson 38: Words with uppercase letters 'G', 'L' and 'Q'

In this lesson you will practice writing words using letters and strokes that you've learnt so far. Pay attention to how uppercase letters connect the lowercase ones. Practice writing these words until you'll get comfortable writing them:

Queens Queens Queens

Queens Queens Queens

Lowell Lowell Lowell

Lowell Lowell Lowell

Quincy Quincy Quincy

Quincy Quincy Quincy

Greeley Greeley Greeley

Greeley Greeley Greeley

Laredo Laredo Laredo

Laredo Laredo Laredo

Lesson 39: Uppercase letters 'D', 'E' and 'Z'

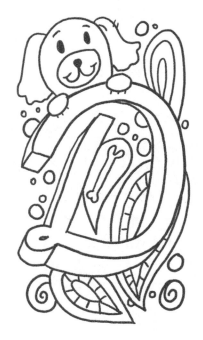

In this lesson you will practice writing words using letters and strokes that you've learnt so far. Pay attention to how uppercase letters connect the lowercase ones. Practice writing these words until you'll get comfortable writing them:

Let's practice writing the letter 'E'. Start at the top line, curve down and to the left, make a little loop at the middle line, then curve down and to the left again:

Now let's practice writing the letter 'Z'. Start near the top line, make a curve that touches the top line and goes halfway between the middle and the bottom line, make a small loop there, curve down below the bottom line, make a loop there and finish with a tail:

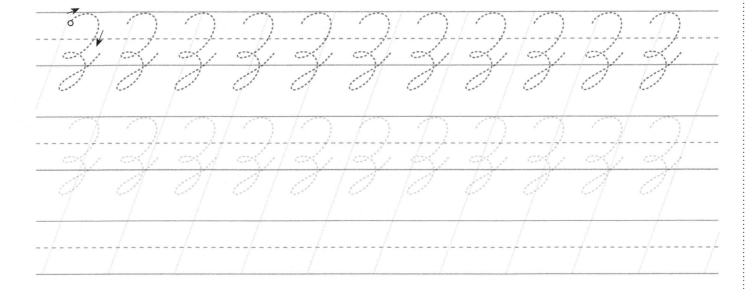

94

Lesson 40: Words with uppercase letters 'D', 'E', and 'Z'

In this lesson you will practice writing words using letters and strokes that you've learnt so far. Pay attention to how uppercase letters connect the lowercase ones. Practice writing these words until you'll get comfortable writing them:

Detroit Detroit Detroit

Detroit Detroit Detroit

Eugene Eugene Eugene

Eugene Eugene Eugene

Zion Zion Zion Zion

Zion Zion Zion Zion

Dayton Dayton Dayton

Dayton Dayton Dayton

Eagan Eagan Eagan

Eagan Eagan Eagan

Lesson 41: Uppercase letters 'I' and 'J'

In this lesson you will learn how to write uppercase letters "I", and 'J'. Let's start with the letter 'I'. Start at the bottom line, pull the stroke up to the top line, make a big loop, then pull the stroke to the left and make a little hook:

Now let's practice writing the letter 'J'. Start at the bottom line, pull up with a big curve that touches the top line, pull down below the bottom line, make a smaller curve there and finish with a little tail:

Lesson 42: Words with uppercase letters 'I' and 'J'

In this lesson you will practice writing words using letters and strokes that you've learnt so far. Pay attention to how uppercase letters connect the lowercase ones. Practice writing these words until they become easy to write:

Idaho Idaho Idaho

Idaho Idaho Idaho

Joliet Joliet Joliet

Joliet Joliet Joliet

Irvine Irvine Irvine

Irvine Irvine Irvine

Jupiter Jupiter Jupiter

Jupiter Jupiter Jupiter

Iselin Iselin Iselin

Iselin Iselin Iselin

Lesson 43: Uppercase letters 'W' and 'X'

In this lesson you will learn how to write uppercase letters "W", and 'X'. Let's start with the letter 'W'. Start with a small hook at the top line, pull down to the bottom line, then up with a little hook, then down again and then up again:

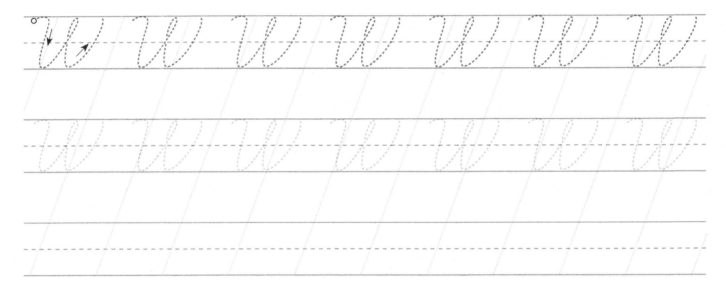

Now let's practice writing the letter 'X'. Start at the top line with a little hook, pull down and to the right, finish that stroke with a tail. Then cross the first stroke from top right to bottom left:

Lesson 44: Words with uppercase letters 'W' and 'X'

In this lesson you will practice writing words using letters and strokes that you've learnt so far. Pay attention to how uppercase letters connect the lowercase ones. Practice writing these words until they become easy to write:

Wichita Wichita

Wichita Wichita

Xenia Xenia Xenia

Xenia Xenia Xenia

Warren Warren Warren

Warren Warren Warren

Xalapa Xalapa Xalapa

Xalapa Xalapa Xalapa

Wheaton Wheaton

Wheaton Wheaton

Congratulations! You've now learnt how to write all the letters of the alphabet in cursive! To finalize your skills let's learn how to write digits!

Lesson 45: Numbers writing practice

Now that you've learned how to write all the uppercase and lowercase letters of the alphabet let's spend some time practicing writing numbers:

Lesson 46: Pangram writing practice

Congratulations! You have now mastered cursive handwriting of all the letters of the alphabet. To celebrate this let's practice writing some pangrams (sentences that contain all the letters of the alphabet).

The quick brown fox

jumps over the lazy dog.

The quick brown fox

jumps over the lazy dog.

The five boxing wizards

jump quickly.

The five boxing wizards

jump quickly.

Zoe and Fred specialise

in the job of making

very quaint wax toys.

Zoe and Fred specialise

in the job of making

very quaint wax toys.

A large fawn jumped
quickly over white
zebras in a box.

A large fawn jumped
quickly over white
zebras in a box.

We quietly gave Bert a

handsome prize for his

six juicy pink plums.

We quietly gave Bert a

handsome prize for his

six juicy pink plums.

Crazy Fredrick bought

many very exquisite

opal jewels.

Crazy Fredrick bought

many very exquisite

opal jewels.

Five or six big jet planes

zoomed quickly past the

tower.

Five or six big jet planes

zoomed quickly past the

tower.

My grandfather picks

up quartz and valuable

onyx jewels.

My grandfather picks

up quartz and valuable

onyx jewels.

sentences
writing practice

Alan asks Amelia about

apricots.

Blair brought books on

bees to Bob.

Crystal cooks creamy
corn chowder.

David delivers delicious
donuts daily.

Elise eats eclairs and eggs
every day.

Florence finished first in
the frog race.

George gave Graham
green goggles.

Hannah has a hairy
hamster named Henry.

Irene ice skates with
Tressa in Illinois.

Jenny just ate John's
jelly beans from a jar.

Keina keeps her keys in
the kitchen.

Luke loves little lemurs
and lemmings.

Mason misses mountain
climbing in Montana.

Nolan's niece Nora needs
a new necklace.

Oscar owns the only
olive orchard in town.

Peter pretends preparing
for philosophy exam.

Quentin ate quite a bit of

quiche.

Robin reads books about

running rabbits.

Sean sees something
slithering in the sand.

Tobin tends to try new
things on Tuesdays.

Usher urges Uwe to get

under an umbrella.

Vincent visited Valerie

for vacation in Venice.

Winston wishes winters

were warmer.

Xavier xeroxed old

X-rays for Xenia.

Yuri eats yummy
yougurt and and yolks.

Zara zigzagged to the
zoo to see the zebras.

Blank writing Practice Sheets

133

Made in the USA
Coppell, TX
25 February 2023

13377642R00077